Battlegan
ARMADA!

A Purnell Book

Written and devised by
Jon Sutherland
and
Simon Farrell

Illustrations and cover by
Peter Dennis

First published in Great Britain in 1988 by
Macdonald & Co (Publishers) Ltd
Greater London House Hampstead Road London NW1 7QX
a Pergamon Press plc company

ISBN 0 361 07970 2

Printed in Great Britain by Purnell Book Production Ltd
a member of BPCC plc

War at sea

Ships have been used as weapons of war for thousands of years. Sea battles have changed the course of history, and decided the fate of empires. One of the most famous victories was that over the great Armada in the summer of 1588, when superior ships, skill, and luck with the weather enabled the commanders of the English fleet to inflict a crushing, humiliating defeat on the Spanish fleet.

Over the centuries before the Armada, fighting ships and the way sea battles were fought were gradually changing. Shipbuilders developed new types of ships and weapons, while sailors found new ways to use the new ships to the best fighting advantage. But until the invention of steam engines in the 19th century, ships were powered either by men rowing or by the force of wind blowing against sails.

Of course, all these ships were only as good as the men who sailed them. The English fleet's victory in 1588 was partly due to the skill of its commanders. Play the game in this book and see if you can match their skill!

Ships of long ago

Muscle-powered ships

The earliest fighting ships were human-powered. They were often rowed by slaves, or sometimes convicts, chained to their seats to stop them running away. It was apallingly hard work, and very boring, too! Some human-powered ships had a sail that could be put up if the wind was in the right direction, but, mostly, the unfortunate rowers had to provide the power. These ships were called galleys, and sailed on the calm Mediterranean sea. Fighting galleys were not very different from ordinary merchant galleys; instead of cargoes of wine and olive oil, they carried soldiers.

Sea battles were much the same as land battles. The enemy soldiers tried to board each others' ships, and then fought to the death with swords and daggers. If they couldn't get close enough to board, then they rained spears and arrows down on the enemy from the galley's deck.

As well as carrying troops to war, or soldiers to board and capture other ships, galleys could also be used as weapons. Each galley was armed with a terrifying bronze battering ram, fixed to the prow (front) of the ship. To attack, the oarsmen rowed as hard as they could to work up top speed. Ancient Greek galleys, powered by 170 oarsmen, could probably reach a maximum speed of 9 knots (about 16½ kilometres per hour). The helmsman steered the galley straight at the enemy ship, trying to hit it broadside on. With luck, the ram would smash a hole in the enemy's hull, sinking it in minutes. Often as not, the rowers could not escape from their chains, and drowned with their ship. A double blow against the enemy!

For defence, galleys copied tactics used on land. There, soldiers arranged themselves into a tight circle, facing outwards, with their spears bristling to confront the enemy. No wonder people called this the 'hedgehog' formation! At sea, galleys also gathered in a circle, with battering rams facing outwards, threatening to dart out and ram any enemy ship that dared to come close enough to attack.

A section and side view of a galley to show how the oarsmen were seated. This galley has three banks of rowers and was called a *trireme* by the Greeks. A *bireme* was a two-banked galley. In any sort of galley it was essential that the oarsmen kept perfect time with each other. A rower who missed his stroke would probably break several other oars and could severely injure himself. To try and prevent this, a Greek galley's crew would include a flute-player who piped time for the rowers.

A Greek galley rams a Persian galley in battle.

The Roman navies

While Roman soldiers ruled the land, their ships conquered the seas. The Romans had a well-trained and superbly disciplined army and navy. Their engineers developed ingenious machines to help them win wars on land, and began to make changes to their ships, as well, to make them more effective in battle. They built towers on the decks, for archers to fire from, and armour-plated their galleys, for protection when they were rammed. To help their soldiers board and capture enemy ships more easily, they invented a strange device called a *corvus*. This was a strong wooden plank with a huge metal spike at one end, pointing downwards. As the attacking galley pulled alongside its chosen target, its sailors swung the *corvus* out over the water, and lowered the spiked end on to the enemy's deck. The spike sank into the deckboards, 'nailing' the two ships together. The Roman soldiers could then leap across to attack the enemy crew.

Even the greatest empires come to an end, and eventually the Roman Empire collapsed. There was no longer one supreme power in Europe, just a collection of warring states. There were no great generals to

The *corvus* of a Roman galley enabled the Romans to use their mighty infantry even at sea.

organize new campaigns, or to plan and fight great battles at sea. No-one encouraged inventors to design new ships, or new machines for fighting. But in the far north, a new power was rising. Soon, terrified women and children were shouting in panic: 'Vikings! Help! Save us! The raiders are coming from the sea!'

The Vikings were fierce warriors and skilful sailors. It seems likely that they even rowed and sailed their heavy longboats across the northern Atlantic to America. But they fought most battles on land. If they did fight at sea, like the Romans, they either fired spears and arrows across the water, or brought their ships alongside each other and fought hand-to-hand. It was not until the sixteenth century that new fighting ships and a new way of fighting at sea, were developed. In defeating the Spanish Armada, the English showed just how effective these ships and this new way of fighting could be.

Wind-powered ships

Sailing ships, which caught the wind in their sails, were not new in the sixteenth century. Galleys and Viking longboats had sails, although they were not very useful. Their sailors still relied on muscle-power to take the ship where it needed to go. But long before the time of the Armada, single-sailed cargo ships, called 'cogs', were developed to sail in rough northern waters. They had stronger, deeper hulls than southern galleys and used the power of the wind to drive them along. They had a few oars to help them move in a calm, but they were too slow and heavy to row for long, and their masters wanted to fill their holds with cargo, not with slaves bent over their oars, and food to feed them. Cargo was more profitable! If a cog got into a fight, then its master sent archers to the highest points of the deck to fire arrows at the enemy, and, like the Romans and Vikings before him, made ready to repel boarders!

New ships and new ways of fighting

New ships

Different types of sailing ships were built for different purposes; some for local trade, others for long ocean voyages. At first, there was little difference between merchant ships and fighting ships. Most large ships carried weapons of some sort, and perhaps a few soldiers to protect the passengers. But gradually, during the sixteenth century, specialized ships (called 'carracks') were built, to carry cargo back to Europe from the New World (the Americas). People soon realised that these clumsy ships were far too slow and cumbersome for use in battle, and so new fighting ships, called galleons, were designed. They were faster, sleeker, and very manoeuvrable, thanks to the improved arrangement of their sails, and their streamlined hull shape. All these features made them much more useful in battle than the fragile galleys or the lumbering carracks.

New weapons

It was not just their speed and manoeuvrability that made galleons such good fighting ships. They were designed to carry guns! By the sixteenth century, gunsmiths had discovered how to make cannon suitable for taking on board ship. Some early sixteenth-century sailing ships had been converted to warships by having rows of holes, called gun-ports, cut along their sides for the guns to fire out from.

At first, the new guns could not fire their shot very far, and it was difficult to aim them accurately. Even so, they were still deadly weapons. They could kill or maim several men at once and punch gaping holes in an enemy ship's side, all from a distance. It was no longer necessary to board a ship to destroy it. Captains developed new sailing skills to make the best use of their new guns in battle. With a fast ship, like a galleon, a skilful captain could sail to within firing

Sea battles in Medieval times were still little more than land battles fought on water. The high 'castles' at the stern and bow of a ship were designed to give an advantage in hand-to-hand fighting and longer-range archery.

Early cannon were built up with iron strips bound with iron hoops. They were very dangerous and were liable to blow up! Cannon cast in solid bronze were much safer but more expensive to make. The battles of the Armada were fought with a mixture of both cannons.

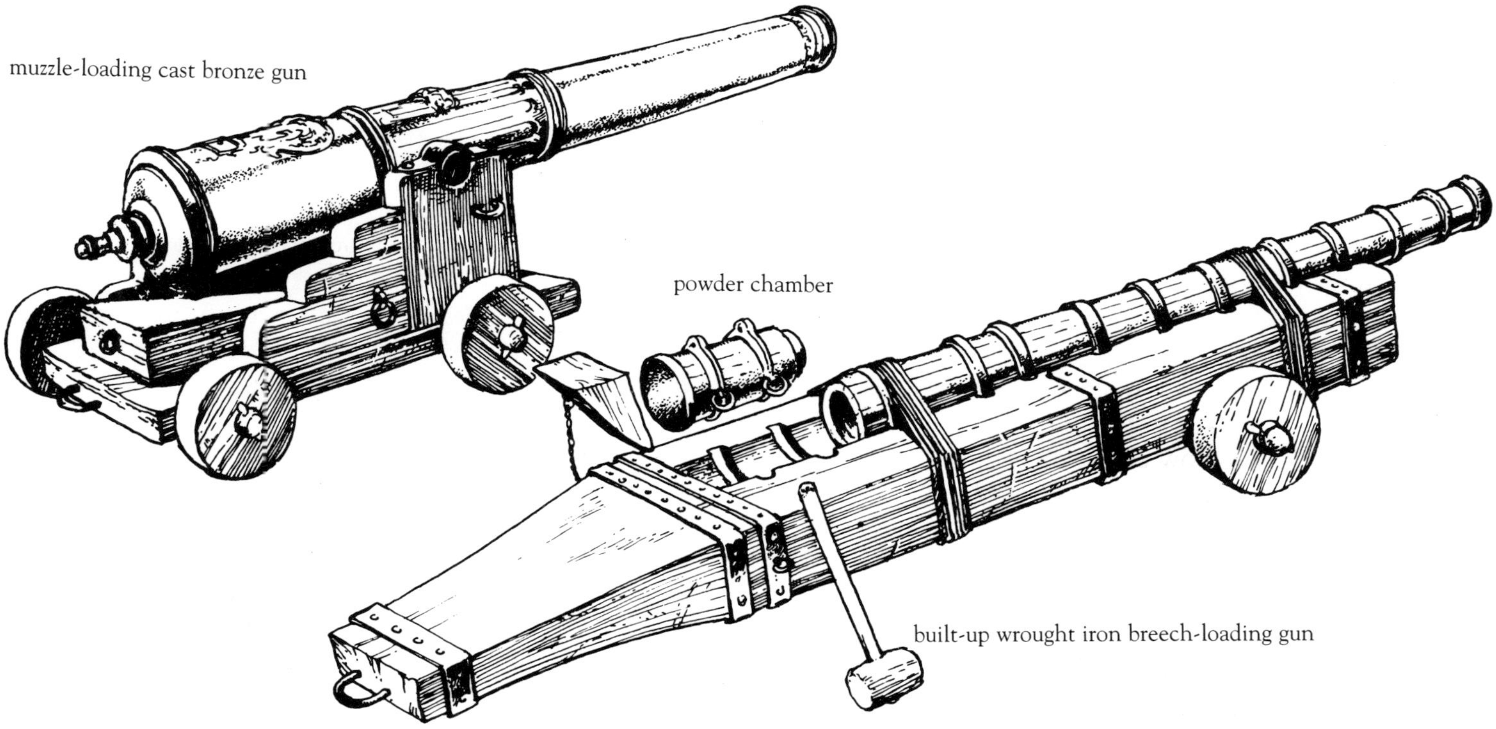

range of his enemy, deliver a furious 'broadside' of shots at his target, and then veer away, before the enemy had a chance to fire back. It took courage, daring and good seamanship to be able to do this. But in the battles that the Spanish Armada was defeated at, the English captains showed that they possessed these qualities. When you play the Armada game, will you be able to handle your fleets as well?

Wind-powered ships could be used as weapons in another way. They could be turned into fireships by cramming them full of anything that would burn – old rope, straw, sawdust, pitch and tar – and set on fire. Then they were towed towards the enemy and set adrift. Can you imagine what it must have felt like to see one of these terrifying 'devil ships' approaching you from across the sea?

The defeat of the Spanish Armada

The reasons for war

Hardly any corner of Europe in the sixteenth century was untouched by war. The English fought the French, the Spaniards fought the Portuguese, the Dutch rebelled against their Spanish emperor, and the French, the Italians and the Germans fought among themselves in a series of bitter civil wars. Yet kings and queens didn't want wars. War was bloody, tragic and expensive. It took men away from vital work at home. Invading armies destroyed crops and looted towns. Sometimes they massacred the local population as well. So why did wars break out? What made Queen Elizabeth and King Philip decide in 1588 that their countries must fight?

England and Spain quarrelled for three reasons: religion, piracy and politics. None of these quarrels was new in 1588; they had been rumbling on for 20 years or more. But, by the time the Armada was ready to set sail, both England and Spain felt that each other's behaviour was more than simply quarrelsome – it was becoming a threat. War was necessary, they felt, to defend themselves against that threat.

England felt threatened by King Philip's attempts to make everyone follow his own religious beliefs. Philip was Catholic, Elizabeth was Protestant. Philip therefore saw it as his duty to remove Elizabeth from her throne and to replace her with a Catholic ruler. He tried to do this in three different ways. Firstly he helped to send undercover Catholic missionaries to England; then, with the Pope, he encouraged the Catholics in Ireland to rebel against Elizabeth. Most dangerous of all, he supported the Catholic Mary Queen of Scots in her plotting to become Queen of England.

Spain, in turn, felt threatened by frequent English attacks on her ships and ports, both in Europe and in the New World. Bold sailors, like Francis Drake, attacked Spaniards and their property wherever they could find it and seized vast amounts of gold and precious goods. King Philip suspected that they were secretly encouraged by Queen Elizabeth, and he was probably right. Because of these raids, Spanish trade was disrupted, and the Spanish royal treasury became disastrously short of money. All Spaniards felt humiliated by the daring English attacks.

England and Spain also quarrelled over political alliances, and this was what finally led to war. England was horrified when Spain conquered Portugal, one of England's oldest allies. This conquest made Philip ruler of over half the known world, and doubly dangerous to England. Spain and England supported opposite sides in the French civil wars, and therefore came to regard themselves as enemies in that way, too. And Philip was furious when England sent troops to support the Dutch Protestants who were rebelling against him. At last, the smouldering quarrels burst into flames. Philip agreed with his generals. It was time to invade England. They would send an Armada!

Queen Elizabeth I of England

Who was who in 1588?

Queen Elizabeth I (1534–1603) At the time of the Armada, Elizabeth was 54 years old. She was the second daughter of Henry VIII. She was crowned in 1558, when she was only 24. Despite many problems in her early years as queen, she resisted all attempts to dethrone her.

She was a Protestant, though it is hard to tell how sincere her religious beliefs were, and how much they were affected by politics. She was intelligent and very well-educated: she spoke Latin, Greek, French, German, and Italian, studied history and law, and was fond of music and poetry. She was also vain, cautious, mistrustful, stubborn, penny-pinching, skilled at concealing her real feelings, and an absolutely brilliant politician. She usually managed to get her own way. All the great rulers of Europe, except the Pope, who could not marry, wanted to marry her. That way, they could add England to their empires. But she refused them all, and preserved England's independence by remaining single. Although she was involved in wars with France and then with Spain, she preferred peace to war. Not that she was unpatriotic. Far from it. War cost too much, she said. Too much money and too many men's lives. Unlike Sir Francis Drake, she was not eager to attack Spain, but when she learned of the Spanish plans for the Armada, she allowed her commanders on land and sea to start making preparations for war. When the Armada threatened England, she rallied her troops and encouraged her subjects with a rousing speech at Tilbury.

King Philip II of Spain

King Philip II (1527–1598) At the time of the Armada, Philip was 61 years old. He had become King of Spain in 1556. By inheritance and conquest, he ruled over half the world. The Spanish Empire stretched right round the globe, from Peru in the far west to the Philippines (named after him) far in the east. Philip was a devout Catholic, who felt that, as king, he had a holy task to perform. He was the guardian not only of his subjects' lives, but also of their souls. He felt, too, that it was his duty to try and convert as many people as possible to his faith. In the Spanish colonies, that meant sending missionaries. In Europe, it meant trying to conquer Protestant countries, like England and the Netherlands. He wanted to expand his empire, but, like Queen Elizabeth, he did not want war for its own sake. He had to be persuaded by his generals that attacking England was the right thing to do, and when he did agree to start preparing the Armada, he kept asking them not to spend so much money on ships and provisions. He was a tireless worker, careful, painstaking, precise, often worried, quite unable to delegate work to his assistants, and disastrously slow at making decisions. He did not enjoy being king. He would have preferred to spend his days in prayer and meditation, like a monk, or else quietly at home with his family. Unhappily, fate had given him a different part to play, and he was not well-fitted to perform it.

Sir Francis Drake (1540?–1596) Born into a poor, but fiercely Protestant family, Drake was apprenticed to a sea captain, and quickly became an expert sailor. He joined his cousin John Hawkins on one of his voyages to the West Indies. While there, the Spaniards treacherously massacred Drake's companions. Drake vowed revenge, and asked Queen Elizabeth for her support. She refused to give him official permission to

Sir Francis Drake

attack the Spanish, but probably helped to finance at least one of his raiding voyages. Drake spent most of his life at sea, combining attacks on Spanish colonies and treasure ships with heroic adventures and bold explorations. Loved and respected by the English, feared and hated by the Spanish, Drake was a brave and daring adventurer.

The Duke of Medina Sidonia

The Duke of Medina Sidonia (1550–1615) A distinguished Spanish nobleman, Medina Sidonia was head of one of the most respected families in Spain. He was appointed to lead the Armada by King Philip. The previous leader had been a professional soldier and sailor, but he died before the Armada was ready. Medina Sidonia was neither a soldier nor a sailor, and pleaded with the king, saying that he was the wrong choice for the job. But Philip insisted that he take it. He knew that all the lesser nobles and captains would obey Medina Sidonia, out of respect for his rank, and, to Philip, that was all that mattered. Philip was wrong. Medina Sidonia did his best, but he was miserably seasick for most of the Armada's voyage, and had to rely on the conflicting advice of his junior officers. He was also deluged with letters of advice from the king. How was he to know the right course of action? He had hardly ever been to sea before! He was sensible, intelligent, cultured, obedient to his king, and totally unsuited to the task of leading the Armada. He gave up a peaceful existence at home to do his duty for his country. Not surprisingly, he made disastrous mistakes, and, when the Armada was defeated, he returned home in disgrace. In serving his king and country, his life had been ruined.

The Duke of Parma (1545–1592) Regarded as the best soldier of his generation, Parma was bold, ambitious, ruthless and efficient. He commanded the Spanish army in the Netherlands. He had been sent there to put down a rebellion by the Dutch Protestants, who were fighting for independence from Spanish rule. He fought a tough war skilfully and with great stamina. Like Medina Sidonia, he was constantly receiving orders and unsuitable advice from the king in far-away Spain. He did not really believe that the king's scheme to invade England would work, although he agreed to try and cooperate with Philip's plans.

Lord Howard of Effingham (1536–1624) A distant cousin of Queen Elizabeth, Howard was appointed commander-in-chief of the fleet that was made ready to attack the Armada. Like Philip of Spain, Elizabeth knew that her captains would obey a high-ranking nobleman. Unlike Philip, she chose a suitable noble for the job! Howard was a decisive man, and used to taking command. He handled his junior officers, including Drake and Hawkins, firmly but tactfully. Acting on their advice, he made good use of his ships, and the shifting winds and tides, to lead the English to victory against the Armada.

Sir John Hawkins

Sir John Hawkins (1532–95) Cousin to Francis Drake, and member of a wealthy West Country ship-owning family. Hawkins was a shrewd, skilful, experienced seaman, and a businesslike administrator. He traded in African slaves and precious goods from the New World, and was one of the richest men in Europe. He took a special interest in ship building and design, and was appointed Treasurer of the Navy by the queen.

Battlegame ARMADA!

Rules

Battlegame Armada! is a game of skill and luck for two players. The 'fleets' in the game are named after some of the main squadron leaders on either side. The result of the game is up to you!

1 Playing Counters

Carefully open the staples of this book and remove the board and counters. Cut out the counters and wind roses for each side.
Spanish counters are red and English counters green. There are two main kinds of counter: fleets and armies. Each army or fleet counter has a number which represents its Fighting Strength ('strength'). Each side also has a fireship counter and a direction-finder arrow counter.
You will need a dice to play the game.

2 Object of the game

Both players take turns to move and attack. A turn begins with a player moving his or her forces and ends when he or she has completed any resulting battles. The other player's turn then begins. Spain wins by occupying London for two Spanish turns *after* defeating any English troops in the city. Victory is only complete if Spain is not attacked by England during these two turns, otherwise Spain must start another occupation for two turns. England wins when Spain has no armies left that can reach London to attack. (Parma's army is useless for a Spanish victory if there are no Spanish fleets to transport it to England).

3 Building the Spanish Invasion Fleet

Players choose sides. Spain takes the two Parma army counters, each with a strength of 10, and places them in Holland on the hexagons ('hexes') marked 'Parma's Army'. Spain then takes the three fleet counters marked M. SIDONIA (60), RECALDE (40), and VALDES (40) and places each one in any of the red hexes at the bottom left of the board. In addition, Spain takes 40 Fighting Strength points worth of Army counters and divides them between the three fleets (e.g. a 20 strength counter for M. Sidonia, a 10 and a 6 [=16] counter for Recalde and a 4 strength counter for Valdes), placing the army counters under the fleet counters. A Spanish army's strength at sea must *never* be more than half the strength of the fleet that transports it.

4 England prepares against the Spanish invasion

When Spain has chosen its forces and placed them in their hexes, England chooses its forces. England takes the six army counters marked 'MILITIA', each with a strength of 4, and places one on each English port *except* London, which is not a port and can only be attacked from land. Note that English ports can be occupied by both armies and fleets. Militia counters cannot move out of their home ports.

England then takes four fleet counters marked HOWARD (40), DRAKE (30), HAWKINS (20), and FROBISHER (20) and places each one in a different English port. England also takes 20 Fighting Strength points worth of army counters and places them anywhere in England. They will defend England; you can divide them up as you wish, scattering them across the country or concentrating them in one hex. English army counters *cannot* be carried by fleets. Never accidentally take the English militia to sea – they get seasick!

5 Playing the Game

Players take turns to move. Spain moves first. On its turn, Spain moves all its forces and then fights any battles which result; then England does the same. Only one fleet and up to 25 Fighting Strength points of troops of the same side may occupy a hex. (A similar strength of the enemy's forces may also occupy the same hex). A fleet cannot be split up into smaller fleets occupying different hexes. Fighting between fleets only happens after the attacking fleets have been moved into position.

6 Wind

Each player, at the start of a turn, throws the dice to work out the strength and direction of the wind. First, roll the dice for the wind strength. Look up the dice number on the Wind Strength Table on the board. This tells you if you are sailing in a Breeze, Stiff Wind or Gale. Now take your country's wind rose for that wind strength. Throw the dice again and place the wind rose on the compass, with its large arrow pointing to the dice number you threw.

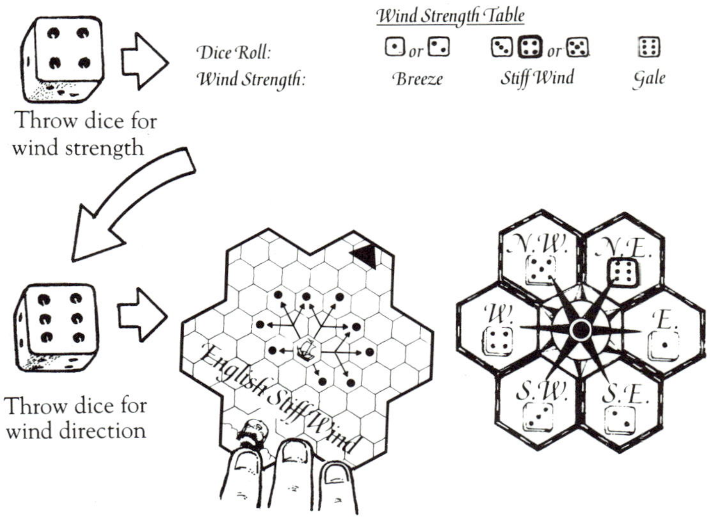

7 How fleets move

Fleets move according to the wind, using a wind rose and compass as shown above. Look at the wind rose to see the different hexes into which your fleets can move. The white hex shows a fleet's position; the large dots show the hexes you can move to. Compare the wind rose with the position of your fleets at sea to make your move – you may find that placing the large direction-finder arrow counter on your fleet helps you work out your possible moves. Now choose the move you wish to make, not forgetting to move *all* your fleets at sea by the same method. Enemy fleets do not move until their turn. You must move your fleets the full number of hexes shown by the wind rose, even if this forces a fleet aground, in which case the fleet and any armies it transports are lost. Fleets may 'pass through' other fleets on their way to new positions.

You'll see that England can always move to more hexes than Spain. This is because in 1588 English ships were more manoeuvrable and could take better advantage of the wind than the Spanish ships could.

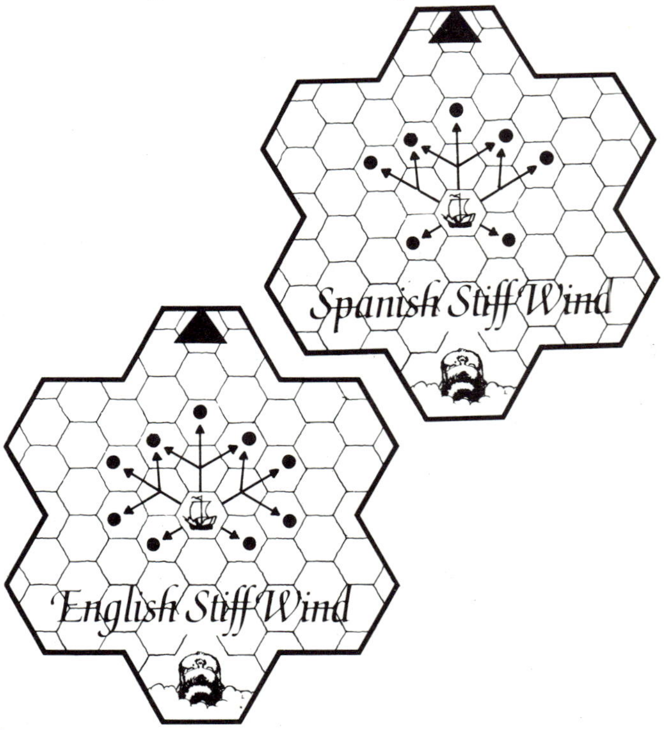

8 How armies move

Spanish armies at sea move with their fleets. Armies on land are not affected by the wind and can move only one hex at a time. They may move in any direction. They may not move into hilly (brown) areas. Armies on land are moved when you move your fleets. You need not move an army if you don't want to.

9 English sea attacks
Only fleets fight at sea. An English fleet can attack a Spanish fleet by moving into the same hex as the Spanish fleet or it can attack from any one of the hexes surrounding the Spanish fleet.
Although a fleet can only make one attack per turn, two or more English fleets can attack the same Spanish fleet from different hexes.

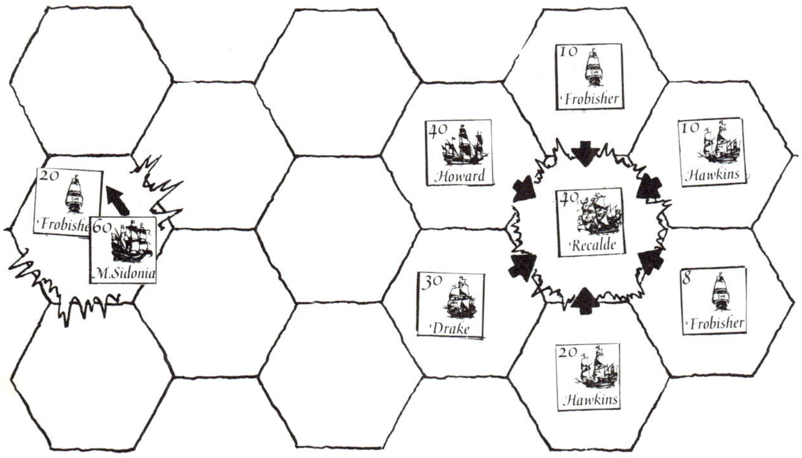

10 Spanish sea attacks
A Spanish fleet can only attack an English fleet when the two fleets are in the same hex.

11 Fighting back
If you are attacked, you will have a chance to fight back when it is your own go. Attacks can only be made after a player completes all his or her land and sea moves.

12 Battle damage
Fleets fight with their Fighting Strength. The way you do this is simple: check the Fighting Strength of your fleet and roll the dice. Look at the Combat Results Table on the board, and look across the row for the number you threw. Now look down the column that includes the Fighting Strength of your fleet. Where the dice row and Fighting Strength column meet shows how much you have damaged the enemy; your enemy must reduce the strength of his or her fleet by this amount, and replace the damaged counter with a new, lower one. Round up any odd numbers that result. A damaged Spanish fleet with an army must also reduce its army strength to no more than half the fleet's reduced strength.

Combat Results Table

Dice Roll	Attacking Forces Fighting Strength							
	1-6	7-12	13-18	19-24	25-30	33-36	37-42	45-50
1	0	2	4	6	8	10	12	14
2	2	4	6	8	10	12	14	16
3	4	6	8	10	12	14	16	18
4	6	8	10	12	14	16	18	20
5	8	10	12	14	16	18	20	22
6	10	12	14	16	18	20	22	24

13 Fighting on land
Only armies fight on land. Armies can only attack each other when they are both in the same hex, no matter which side is attacking. Fight your land battles after you have completed any sea battles. Use the Combat Results Table in the same way as for fleets.

14 Disembarking troops
Spanish troops can only disembark (get off a fleet) at a port. A fleet can only enter a port if a move shown on a wind rose ends in the port. If there is an English army or militia in the port, the Spanish army must attack and defeat it before the Spanish army can disembark: the Spanish army can move onto the mainland hex, and the fleet into open sea, on the turn after all the defending troops have been defeated. If there are no defending troops in the port, the Spanish army and fleet may move out of the port on the turn after they arrive.

15 Embarking Parma's army from Holland (Spanish Provinces)
The water is too shallow on the Dutch coast for a Spanish fleet to get into a port. Instead, a Spanish fleet must wait three turns in the shallow (yellow) water along the Dutch coast. Since the fleet is still affected by the wind, this means that at the end of each turn, the Spanish fleet must end its wind move in a yellow hex. If it does not, the Spanish fleet must start again. Parma's army can move along the purple hexes one at a time, to try and keep up with the waiting fleet. When the fleet picks up the army at the start of the fourth turn, the fleet must be in a hex next to the army.
If your fleet strength is not enough to carry a 10 strength Army, you cán split the army into smaller units – use ordinary Spanish army counters for this.

16 Attacking while embarking or disembarking
Spanish fleets on the Dutch coast or in an English port can be attacked while they are embarking or disembarking; a Spanish fleet may defend itself but if it is damaged *before* it has disembarked its troops, the army is reduced in the normal way to no more than half the fleet strength.

17 Sheltering in ports
Ships are not affected by the wind when in port. Fleets can shelter in neutral French ports, where they cannot be attacked. Fleets may shelter in English ports while they wait for a favourable wind to take them away, but they can still be attacked. No fleet may stay in any port for more than three turns – on the fourth, it must move out, regardless of the weather, even if this means the fleet is blown aground.

18 Fireships
Each player has one fireship counter that can be used only once in the game. Fireships can be used against ships *anywhere* on the board. A player launches a fireship from a fleet upwind of the enemy, which means a fireship can only travel in a straight line in the direction the wind blows (shown by the large arrow on the wind rose). The fireship can travel the maximum number of hexes shown on the wind rose. It can damage the first fleet it meets in its path. To discover what damage is done, throw a dice and look up the number on the Fireship Table on the board.

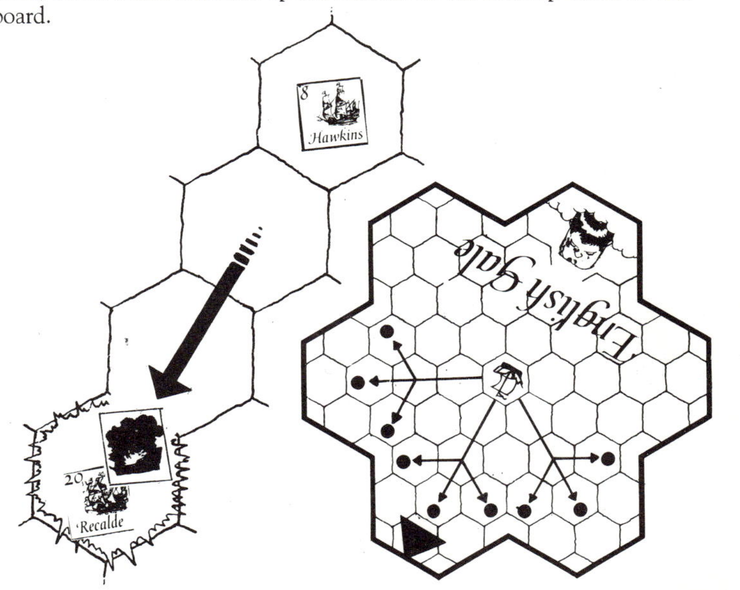

19 Movement off the map
Any fleets blown off the map are lost for ever.

20 Combining fleets
Two damaged fleets whose strengths have each been reduced to ten or less, can be combined to make one stronger fleet by moving the two fleets into the same hex. You must appoint a joint commander and replace the two smaller fleets with one larger fleet.

21 Rescuing Spanish troops at sea
If a Spanish fleet is completely destroyed, any troops it is carrying remain in the water for two turns. If another Spanish fleet can reach their hex in time and has enough fleet strength, some or all of these shipwrecked troops can be rescued.

The Spanish prepare for war

The Spanish Admiral, the Marquis of Santa Cruz, wrote urgently to King Philip to urge him to launch an attack on England. Cautious as ever, Philip sent him away to prepare detailed plans for an invasion, and to find out how much it would cost. Santa Cruz calculated that he would need an enormous fleet of 510 vessels that would carry 64,000 troops.

Even the richest man in the world, which Philip was, could not afford it. But Queen Elizabeth's recent alliance with his Dutch enemies, and Drake's attacks on Spanish ships and settlements in the New World, made Philip agree with Santa Cruz that something had to be done. Reluctantly, he gave orders to start preparing for war.

Soon, the sound of sawing and hammering rang out through the great naval dockyard at Lisbon, as shipwrights and carpenters hurried to build new fighting ships and repair old ones. Philip's agents bought ships from as far away as Germany to swell the fleet, and even seized some unlucky English trading ships that happened to be in Spanish ports. Recruiting-sergeants worked hard to find crews to sail in the new ships, and soldiers to defend them.

All this activity was meant to be a secret, but it was impossible to stop Queen Elizabeth and her spies from discovering what was going on. Spain's plans seemed pretty clear. They were aiming at a two-pronged attack; by the great Armada itself, sailing from Spain, and by the Duke of Parma's crack, battle-hardened troops, conveniently based just across the Channel from England in the Low Countries. For the moment, Parma had his hands full fighting the Dutch rebels, who had been recently been joined by companies of English soldiers. But, given notice, he could march to Dunkirk with his men, rendezvous with the Armada, and launch a combined attack on the flat, poorly-defended south-east coast of England.

England prepares to defend herself

Of course, Queen Elizabeth was not pleased when she heard the news of all this Spanish activity; but she was not dismayed, either. Thanks to Hawkins's reorganization, the English navy was in better shape than it had been for many years. Several new fighting galleons had not long been completed. Francis Drake called one of them, the *Revenge*, 'the perfect warship'. All were strong, fast, and well-armed with guns. There were plenty of merchant ships, and smaller, coastal vessels that could be commandeered in an emergency.

Unlike Philip, the Queen did not arrange to fill her ships with provisions well in advance of any attack, only to see them become rotten and spoilt. Nor did she recruit hundreds of sailors, and keep them hanging about on crowded, verminous ships, only to see many die from diseases before the enemy fired a shot.

England needed an 'early warning system' to alert and ready her ships and men to the danger of the approaching Armada. With no radio, telephones, or fast land transport, the only way to do this was with a network of beacons criss-crossing the country. At the first sight of the Armada off Cornwall, a beacon could be lit, the smoke of which would be seen by the next watchers along the line, who would light their own beacon, and so on down the line. In this way news would travel extremely quickly.

Rather, she made her commanders work out detailed plans for what to do once an attack was launched on England, and then sat back to wait. There would be a panic to get everything ready at the last minute, she knew, but her ways were less expensive, less wasteful and far more flexible than Philip's slow, careful plans.

For defence on land, the queen knew that her subjects were loyal, and that they would eagerly join in the fight against a Spanish invasion. Local gentlemen were ordered to organize townsmen and villagers into well-armed and well-trained corps – rather like a 'Dad's Army.'

Her commanders were not altogether happy with these arrangements. Both Drake and Hawkins begged her to let them make sudden raids on Spain, to destroy what they could of the invasion force and terrorize the local people. The queen had no objections to them harassing Spain 'unofficially', but she still hoped that Philip might cancel his invasion plans. She did not want war if she could avoid it. She feared that an unprovoked attack would give Philip just the excuse he needed to invade England. Hawkins was allowed to set sail with about one-fifth of the English ships in 1586, but the queen's delay in granting him permission to do so spoiled his chances of achieving much.

In 1587, the year before the Armada finally sailed, Drake decided to take a chance. Suspecting that the queen would not approve of what he was about to do, he set off from Plymouth before a royal messenger forbidding him to sail could reach him from London. He sailed to the Spanish coast, and launched a daring raid on Cadiz. He took his ships right into the harbour, destroyed and burned about 30 Spanish ships, and then retreated. His proud boast was that he had 'singed the King of Spain's beard.' Certainly he had made Spain the laughing stock of Europe, and destroyed many valuable ships. Next he sailed on to the Portuguese coast (part of the Spanish empire), captured the castle at Sagres and, for several weeks, used this as a base to terrorize passing ships from. They were mostly cargo boats, laden with wood to make barrels, and provisions for the great Armada. Because of Drake's efforts, many of the Armada ships ran short of essential supplies during their voyage. Finally, he ambushed a massive ship, laden with treasures from the East Indies, before it could get safely home to Spain. It was another severe blow to King Philip; he needed all the money he could get to continue building and equipping the Armada.

Problems for the Armada

At long last, the Armada ships were ready to sail. But two problems still worried Philip, as he paced up and down in his gloomy study. Firstly, would the Armada manage to meet Parma's troops off Dunkirk?

There were several reasons why it might prove tricky. Parma and his men could hardly turn their backs on the Dutch rebels and set off for England without giving the Dutch a fantastic chance to take back all the lands that Parma had fought so hard to capture. Being based in enemy territory, Parma would find it hard to obtain all the barges he needed to ferry his men across the Channel. These barges would have to have an armed escort, too, to protect them from attacks by Dutch Protestant pirates. Could Parma arrange this? The Dutch knew every bay and creek along the coast, and could dart among the enemy barges in their fast, nimble 'flyboats', sniping at the troops on board. The great ships of the Armada could not come close to the shore to defend Parma's barges, because the water was too shallow, and full of lethal shoals and sandbanks. Then there was the problem of sending messages between Parma and the Armada captains. The seas would be full of hostile shipping, both Dutch and English. And messages from Spain – Philip was sure to have second or even third thoughts – could take weeks to get there. How was Parma to know just what he was expected to do? Philip dictated yet another memo to his commanders, and prayed that God would guide them.

The second problem that worried Philip was even more important. Who could he find to take command of the Armada now that Admiral Santa Cruz was dead? Santa Cruz had been a brilliant sea commander. He died in February 1588, when the Armada was almost ready to sail. There seemed to be no-one suitable to take his place. Without a commander, the Armada preparation came to a halt. Men deserted, and supplies went bad or were used up on board the ships still in docks. No-one seemed to know what they should be doing.

King Philip chose a very grand nobleman, the Duke of Medina Sidonia, as the new commander. He knew nothing about ships or the sea; even going out in a

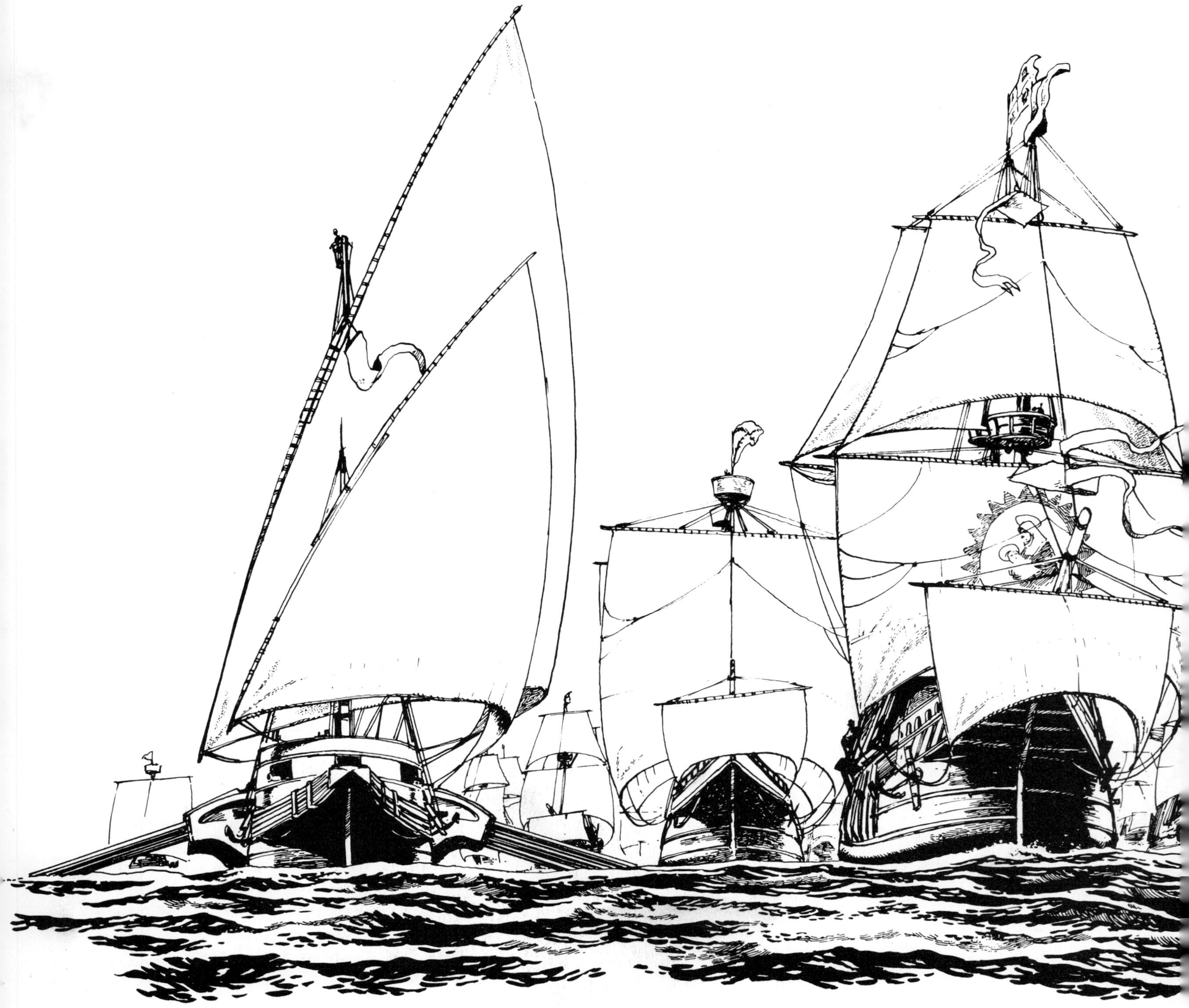

rowing boat made him seasick! Who can tell what might have happened if Santa Cruz had lived to lead the Armada he had worked so hard to prepare?

Spanish and English ships

Although Santa Cruz had asked for enormous numbers of ships when he was planning the Armada, only about 130 ships actually set sail from Lisbon to invade England. Of these, about 30 were purpose-built warships. The rest were converted merchant ships, troop carriers, supply ships and smaller ships for taking messages or spying on the enemy. This fleet was sailed by about 8,000 seamen, and carried about 20,000 soldiers to defend the ships if necessary, and join up with Parma's troops off Dunkirk. Drake's raid on Cadiz, where his guns had smashed the Spanish galleys before they could get close enough to ram him, had proved to the Spaniards that galleys were of little use for modern warfare, but they still brought four with them as part of the fleet. However, rough waves had threatened to swamp the galleys as soon as they entered the Bay of Biscay, and they limped home.

The English fleet contained about the same number of specialist fighting ships, plus a host of local craft of all shapes and sizes, ranging from ocean-going merchant ships to tiny fishing boats. All joined in to help defeat the Spaniards. The English fleet was divided into two, the western squadron, stationed at Plymouth and commanded by Drake, and the eastern squadron, anchored off Sussex, commanded by Lord Howard of Effingham, ably assisted by Hawkins.

So, in some ways, the fleets were evenly matched. Both were equipped with galleons carrying modern guns. Spanish galleons had heavier cannon than the English ships, but the English cannon could fire their

The stately Spanish galleons sailing in close formation up the English Channel must have been an awe-inspiring sight.

shot further. Spanish ships were also filled with soldiers who would easily overwhelm any enemy ship they boarded – if they ever got close enough! But the Spanish galleons were slower and more cumbersome than the English ones, especially because of their higher 'castles' (tiers of decks) at the bow and stern. The English galleons could sail more easily against an opposing wind, and this gave them, if skilfully handled, an enormous advantage when chasing the enemy ships or coming in close to fire. The English were also sailing in familiar waters, and were much closer to their home bases for repairs or supplies.

The hull of a typical English fighting ship in 1588. It shows the lower castles at the stern and bow, while the fish suggests the streamlined hull shape that enabled the English ships to move through the water much faster than the unwieldy Spanish galleons.

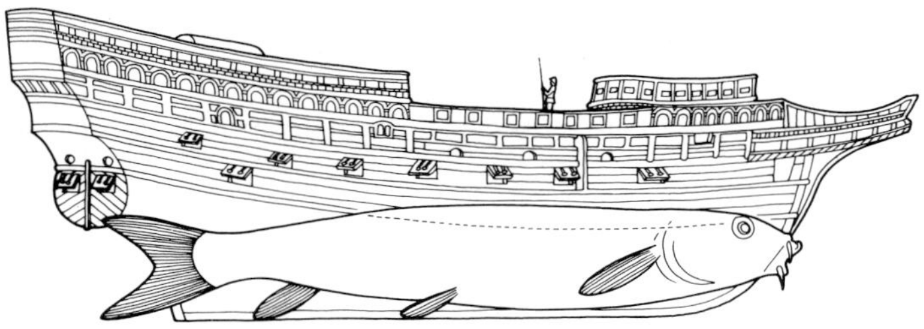

The Armada sets sail

At last the fleet was ready! On 9 May, 1588 the great Armada sailed out of the harbour at Lisbon. But the weather was against it. Fierce gales tossed and buffeted the ships, and they had to wait for nearly three weeks before they could start out to sea. By 1 June they were headed northwards towards England, but progress was slow – sometimes no more than 16 kilometres a day – because the whole fleet had to travel at the pace of the slowest ship.

By 19 June, they had arrived off the northern Spanish port of Corunna. Already the sailors were complaining of rotten, stinking food and filthy drinking water. The food storage barrels were mouldy and leaking; they had been made of soft new wood because Drake's raids on Spanish shipping had destroyed all Spain's stocks of properly prepared wood. Worse still, fever and sickness raged on board the Armada ships. The Spanish decided to call into Corunna for fresh supplies. But that night, a fearful storm hit the coast; the Armada ships were scattered helplessly by the driving wind. Miraculously, none was lost, but many were severely damaged. Medina Sidonia wrote to King Philip, suggesting that it might be better to wait until next year, but the king was stubborn. The Armada must sail!

So, on 21 July, the fleet set sail again. This time, the wind was with them, and they arrived off the Scilly Isles on 29 July. Local rumour had it that a breathless messenger brought the news of their sighting to Drake as he was playing a game of bowls. Drake insisted on finishing his game. He knew that he would not be able to sail out of Plymouth harbour with the wind and tide against him, and that it would be better to let the Spaniards sail past, and then chase them up the Channel.

The English commanders left Plymouth harbour on 30 July. They couldn't help being impressed by the sight that met their eyes. The Armada was magnificent; nearly 130 ships sailing majestically onwards in a tight, defensive, crescent formation. The strongest warships were at the tips of the crescent, and the weakest supply ships in the centre. For the next few days, the English and the Spanish fought a series of battles as the Armada continued its course to meet Parma off Dunkirk. Men were killed and ships damaged on both sides, but neither side could claim to be winning. The English guns had a longer range, and their gunners were more skilful, but they couldn't manage to break the Spanish defensive crescent formation. When they tried to pick off one of the weaker ships, the Spanish galleons rushed to its aid, threatening to trap the English attacking inside the crescent. But when they went on the attack, the Spanish couldn't get close enough to the English ships to seize and board them, as they would have liked to. The English ships were too quick, and their gunners too good, for that. It was stalemate!

For much of the journey up the English Channel, the Armada held a tight crescent formation, with heavily-armed galleons at the edges protecting the weak supply ships in the centre. The English ships (at the left) were unable to inflict any real damage until they broke this defensive formation.

From 2–6 August, the two fleets sailed on. There were battles off Weymouth and the Isle of Wight. As they approached Calais, Medina Sidonia became increasingly worried. Where was Parma? Was he ready? What would happen if they could not join forces? Also, Medina Sidonia was getting dangerously short of ammunition. The English, also, had used enormous quantities of gunpowder and shot, but they could always get new stocks from their home ports. On 6 August, both fleets anchored off Calais. Medina Sidonia sent an urgent message to Parma, who was 50 kilometres away at Dunkirk. Could he send flyboats to help defend the Armada while it rode at anchor? Without them, the Spanish fleet was trapped between the English fleet and the French coast. (The Mayor of Calais had made it clear that he was not going to help either side.)

Fireships struck terror in the hearts of sailors – fire was one of the greatest dangers they faced, for a wooden ship, where almost everything on board would burn, could rapidly turn into a blazing inferno. Although the English fireships did no damage to the Armada, they panicked the Spanish commanders into breaking away from their defensive formation.

Parma could not send any flyboats. He had only a few and, together with his troop-carrying barges, they were trapped inside Dunkirk harbour by the Dutch rebels. Imagine how Medina Sidonia must have felt! So near and yet so far from the all-important meeting! Why wasn't Parma better prepared? Would the planned invasion of England be a failure?

Worse was to come. On 7 August, late at night, the English hastily prepared eight fireships, and towed them towards the Spanish fleet. The wind did the rest of their work for them. The terrifying ships were driven unstoppably on, towards the Armada. Most of the Spanish captains panicked at the sight. They cut their anchor cables and headed for the open sea. At last, the Spanish defensive formation was broken! This was the chance the English had been waiting for!

Next morning, 8 August, revealed a sorry sight. The burnt-out fireships lay harmlessly on the French shore. One of the Spanish galleasses (a cross between a galleon and galley), the *San Lorenzo*, lay shipwrecked outside the harbour. The rest of the Spanish fleet had scattered in disorder. The English were quick to attack. Following Drake's example, they rounded on target ships, smashing them with gunfire and, by skilful seamanship, preventing the Spaniards from getting away from the treacherous coastal waters and regrouping on the open sea. It was a brutal, bloody attack. Many Spanish ships were damaged, and hundreds of Spanish lives lost. As night fell, the English commanders began to feel grimly satisfied.

The main battles and the course of the Spanish Armada up the English Channel. On 29 July 1588 the Armada was first sighted off Cornwall: on 9 August Medina Sidonia decided to retreat, having lost the decisive Battle of Gravelines.

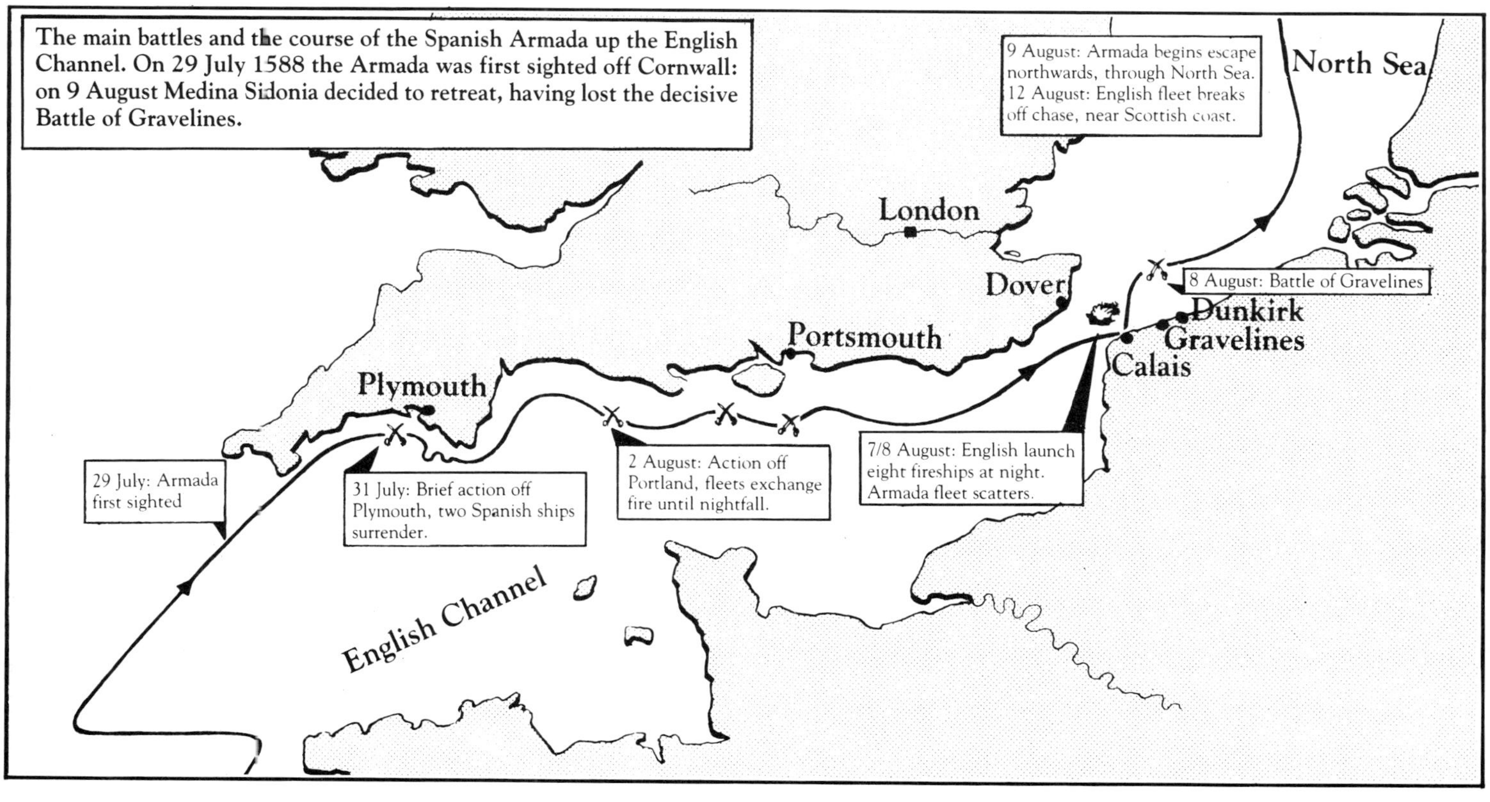

A severely damaged Spanish galleon limps home after defeat at the hands of the weather and the skill of English commanders sailing their superior ships.

An English victory seemed even more certain the next morning. Overnight, the wind had changed to a strong north-westerly. The English knew what that meant. The Spanish ships would be powerless to sail against it out to sea. All the English had to do was watch as the wind drove them to destruction on the sandbanks off Gravelines. On board the ships of the Armada, Spanish sailors fell to their knees in prayer, convinced that their last hour had come. Only a miracle could save them! Then, amazingly, that miracle happened. Suddenly, the wind changed! The Spanish ships limped thankfully out to sea, with the English still pursuing them.

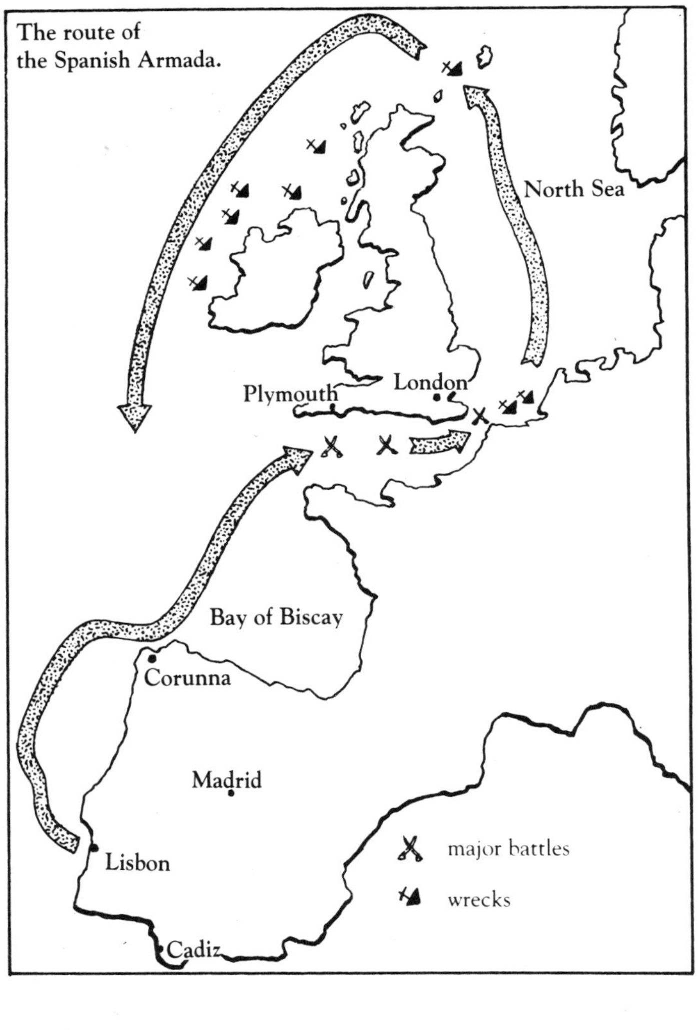

The route of the Spanish Armada.

The voyage home

The Spanish fleet struggled onwards through unfamiliar seas. The English finally gave up the chase off the east coast of Scotland. Medina Sidonia held a council of war, and decided that the Armada should try and make its way back to Spain. But they could not go back the way they had come; the wind was against them and the seas were full of hostile ships. Instead, they decided to sail north and west around Scotland and Ireland.

Together, the Armada ships sailed northwards until they reached the Orkneys. There, a terrible storm scattered the fleet and sank several ships. The battered survivors set course for home as best they could. Some tried to sail through the Irish Sea, but were blown onto rocks off the Scottish and Irish coasts. Many were wrecked. Others sailed down the west coast of Ireland; they too were wrecked when they got too close to the dangerous, unknown shores. Most of the few survivors who managed to reach land were killed by English soldiers, stationed in Ireland. On board ship, men died from starvation or disease.

By September 1588, the weak, sickly survivors of the great Armada straggled pitifully into Corunna harbour. It was four months since they had left with such high hopes. Of the ships and men who had sailed with them, less than half the ships, and only a quarter of the men, returned. King Philip's dream had ended in a nightmare of death and destruction.